HOW TO OVERCOME AVOIDANT PERSONALITY DISORDER

REVOLU

Révolu SAS, 91 rue du Faubourg-Saint-Honoré, 75008 Paris cedex, France

© 2023 Révolu All rights reserved.

Practitioners and researchers must always rely on their own experience and knowledge to evaluate and use any information, methods, compounds, or experiments described herein. Due to the rapid advancement of medical sciences, in particular, independent verification of diagnoses and drug dosages must be performed. To the fullest extent permitted by law, Révolu, the authors, collaborators, or other contributors disclaim any liability for the translation or for any injury and/or damage to persons or property, whether resulting from product liability, negligence, or otherwise, or from the use or application of any methods, products, instructions, or ideas contained in this publication.

The Intellectual Property Code prohibits copies or reproductions intended for collective use. Any representation or reproduction, in whole or in part, by any means whatsoever, without the consent of the author or his/her successors or assigns, is unlawful and constitutes an infringement punishable by articles L335-2 and following of the Intellectual Property Code.

Handbook of Applied Psychology

Introduction

Avoidant personality disorder remains a condition that is still misunderstood by many. Yet, it is one of the psychological realities that some people face, often without knowing it. In this book, we delve into the depths of this disorder, seeking to unravel its mysteries and provide better understanding to those who are confronted by it, either closely or remotely.

Avoidant personality disorder is defined primarily by a profound feeling of inferiority, coupled with a hypersensitivity to rejection. This combination leads to avoidance of social situations for fear of criticism or judgement. Individuals suffering from it tend to see themselves as socially inept, undesirable or inferior to others. It is therefore often difficult for them to interact with others, even in mundane daily life circumstances.

It is imperative to distinguish this disorder from ordinary moments of shyness or insecurity that anyone can feel. Where shyness is temporary, avoidant personality disorder is constant over time. It shapes the individual's perception of themselves and the world around them. As a result, their life can be greatly affected, both professionally and personally.

One question arises: why is it so essential to talk about avoidant personality disorder? The answer lies in its impact. If undiagnosed or untreated, this disorder can lead to extreme loneliness, or even total isolation. Moreover, although the affected person possesses skills, talents or even above average aptitudes, their distorted self-perception can prevent them from fully leveraging these. It is therefore crucial to understand its components and implications in order to better apprehend it and ultimately, better support those who suffer from it.

But what are the main characteristics of this disorder? One often notices a tendency to avoid situations where the individual might be criticized or rejected. This avoidance is not only physical; it can also be emotional. Those affected often avoid expressing disagreement, sharing feelings or initiating relationships, for fear of the other's response. Another observable characteristic is reluctance to get involved in new activities or take personal risks. This reluctance stems from fear of ridicule or shame.

The disorder is also marked by excessive self-monitoring. The individual constantly watches themselves, looking for the slightest sign of disapproval or criticism in others' behavior. This hypervigilance is exhausting, both mentally and physically. It keeps the person in a permanent state of tension, where every interaction is analyzed, dissected, judged. The slightest deviation, the subtlest glance can be interpreted as a sign of rejection.

It is easy to understand how paralyzing this condition can be. However, becoming aware of the disorder, its origins and manifestations, is the first step towards better management. Information and knowledge remain the most powerful tools in this quest. By understanding the disorder, perceiving its nuances and subtleties, it becomes easier to confront it head-on.

I want to clarify that avoidant personality disorder is not inevitable. Many people, informed and supported, have succeeded in overcoming their fears and establishing fulfilling relationships. It is therefore crucial not to underestimate the importance of education and information in this process.

Handbook of Applied Psychology

History and Epidemiology

When we delve into the history of psychology and psychiatry, we find that the recognition of personality disorders, particularly avoidant personality disorder, is relatively recent. To understand this evolution, it is necessary to go back in time and revisit certain key milestones that have shaped our current understanding of this disorder.

The emergence of modern psychiatry in the 19th century sparked an interest in the various manifestations of mental pathologies. Yet, for a long time, the classification of disorders was crude. Individuals showing signs of social avoidance or heightened sensitivity were often lumped together with other pathologies, due to a lack of deep understanding of their specificities.

It was only in the 20th century, with the advent of psychoanalysis and the rise of clinical studies, that researchers and practitioners began to differentiate and define personality disorders more precisely. The initial descriptions of avoidant disorder referred to individuals as «hypersensitive» or «avoiding confrontation». However, these characterizations were still vague, and it took several decades for the disorder to be clearly defined and distinguished from other pathologies.

A key milestone in this recognition was the inclusion of avoidant personality disorder in the third edition of the Diagnostic and Statistical Manual of Mental Disorders (DSM) in 1980. This inclusion marked the official recognition of the disorder as a distinct entity, justifying specific research and interventions.

Since then, studies have been launched to better understand the origins, manifestations, and implications of the disorder. These research efforts have been essential in developing precise diagnostic criteria and guiding therapeutic interventions.

Now, turning to the epidemiology of avoidant personality disorder. To grasp the prevalence of this disorder, it is essential to refer to recent studies that attempt to estimate the percentage of the population affected. Although these studies vary by country and methodology used, a general trend can nevertheless be discerned.

The most recent epidemiological studies suggest that avoidant personality disorder affects about 1 to 2.5% of the general population. However, this figure can reach

10% or more in clinical populations, where individuals seek help for psychological problems. It is noteworthy that these figures are estimates, and the actual prevalence may be slightly different.

Several factors can influence the prevalence of this disorder. For example, cultural differences play a significant role. In some cultures, behaviors associated with the avoidant disorder might be less visible or interpreted differently. Moreover, the disorder could be underdiagnosed, as many individuals avoid contact with the healthcare system for fear of judgment.

Furthermore, some studies have examined the prevalence of the disorder by sex. Although the results are not unanimous, the majority suggest that the disorder is slightly more common in women than in men.

It is also crucial to mention that the prevalence of avoidant personality disorder can vary by age. Symptoms may become more apparent in adolescence or early adulthood, but they can also diminish over time for some individuals. This underscores the importance of regular monitoring and appropriate assessment throughout life.

Handbook of Applied Psychology

Potential Causes of the Disorder

The question of the origins of avoidant personality disorder is complex and multifactorial. Attempting to understand the underlying causes of this disorder confronts us with an intertwining of genetic, environmental and developmental factors. For many, the answer lies not in a single factor, but rather in the interaction of several elements. Let's dive into this exploration, drawing on current research and scientific discoveries.

Let's start with genetic factors. Numerous studies suggest that personality disorders in general can have a hereditary component. Although genetics alone cannot be held responsible for the onset of avoidant disorder, it could make some individuals more vulnerable. Studies conducted on twins, in particular, have revealed that when one twin suffers from avoidant personality disorder, the probability that the other twin will also be affected is higher than in the general population.

However, even if this genetic predisposition exists, it does not guarantee at all that the disorder will manifest. This underlines the importance of environmental and developmental factors in the equation.

Speaking of environmental factors, several elements can influence the development of the disorder. Experiences during childhood, such as rejection, ridicule, or humiliation, can contribute to the formation of an avoidant thought pattern. A child who has been regularly criticized or bullied may, over time, develop a deep fear of rejection and a negative view of themselves. This perspective is reinforced if the child has not had the opportunity to have positive or encouraging experiences to counterbalance these difficult moments.

In addition to traumatic experiences, family dynamics play a crucial role. Overprotective parenting, where the child is constantly shielded from challenges or risks, can limit their ability to develop social skills. Conversely, a family environment where the child is constantly under pressure or subject to unrealistic expectations can lead to a fear of failure or judgement.

It is also important to consider the role of developmental factors. Personality development is not static; it evolves over time, influenced by a multitude of experiences and interactions. Adolescence, for example, is a critical period when the individual forges their identity and faces new social challenges. A teenager struggling to fit in or facing repeated rejection may develop avoidant behaviors. In addition, the way an individual learns to manage emotions, understand and respond to social expectations can influence the development of avoidant disorder.

Of course, not all individuals facing negative experiences will develop avoidant personality disorder. Some will manage to overcome these obstacles and build a positive self-image. Others, however, may internalize these experiences, integrating them into their own self-vision and their relationship with others.

It is also necessary to mention that avoidant personality disorder does not necessarily manifest itself from early childhood. Although some signs may be observed early on, the disorder can also manifest later in adulthood, following particular events or situations.

It should also be noted that the manifestation of avoidant personality disorder can be influenced by other coexisting conditions or disorders. For example, someone suffering from depression or anxiety may exhibit exacerbated symptoms of avoidance. Conversely, avoidant disorder itself can exacerbate symptoms of other conditions.

In conclusion, the causes of avoidant personality disorder are far from straightforward. They result from the interaction of genetic, environmental and developmental factors. Although genetic predispositions may exist, they alone do not explain the manifestation of the disorder. Lived experiences, family dynamics, and personal development play equally crucial roles. Understanding these causes is essential for developing tailored interventions and providing adequate support to affected individuals.

Handbook of Applied Psychology

Symptoms and Diagnosis

Avoidant personality disorder is a clinical entity that, while less overt than other psychiatric disorders, has its own distinct characteristics. Mental health professionals rely on a combination of clinical and behavioral manifestations for its recognition. Diagnosing this disorder is crucial to guide the patient towards appropriate treatment, and thus, a deep understanding of its symptoms and criteria is essential.

One of the predominant signs of this disorder is a persistent avoidance of social activities due to the fear of criticism or rejection. This fear is so pervasive that it can paralyze individuals in various situations, preventing them from engaging in numerous activities, whether professional, social, or personal. Surprisingly, these individuals may have a strong desire for social interaction, but this aspiration is overshadowed by a terror of judgment.

This fear of judgment also manifests as a reluctance to share opinions or feelings. Individuals with avoidant personality disorder may fear causing conflict or eliciting disapproval. Thus, they might choose to passively conform to others' opinions or refrain from any comments.

Hyper-sensitivity to negative feedback is also a central symptom. A critique, even if minor and well-intentioned, can be interpreted as a direct attack. This reaction is not merely a susceptibility; it can be felt intensely and cause profound distress.

The self-image of these individuals is often distorted. They may see themselves as socially incompetent, inferior, or unattractive, even if this strongly contrasts with reality. This skewed self-view can stem from previous experiences or an excessive focus on failures or embarrassing moments.

Furthermore, hesitation to form new relationships is a common symptom. The fear of rejection or ridicule can be a significant barrier to establishing new connections. This avoidance behavior can unfortunately be misinterpreted by others as disaffection or indifference.

Another distinctive trait is the constant search for reassurances of acceptance. Before venturing into new situations, whether social or professional, the person may need assurances. They often seek to be reassured that they will not be criticized or rejected.

Establishing a diagnosis requires a comprehensive clinical evaluation conducted by a professional. Structured interviews, questionnaires, and an analysis of history can help distinguish this disorder from other conditions. It is crucial to base the diagnosis on the entire clinical picture and verify the persistence of symptoms, as avoidant personality disorder can sometimes be confused with other disorders, particularly anxiety disorders.

Handbook of Applied Psychology

Common Myths Surrounding the Disorder

The understanding of mental disorders in society is a mix of knowledge, cultural beliefs and stereotypes. Avoidant personality disorder is no exception to this rule. Although continuous efforts are being made to educate the public and demystify personality disorders, misconceptions remain, fueled by ignorance, media or anecdotal testimonies. These myths can have harmful consequences, not only by reinforcing stigma but also by affecting the self-perception of those affected. Let's address these false ideas in order to deconstruct them.

First, a common myth is that avoidant personality disorder is simply an extreme form of shyness. While shyness is a trait that some affected people may exhibit, it is reductive to consider this disorder as a simple exaggeration of shyness. Shyness is usually a fleeting or situational reaction, whereas avoidant personality disorder is a persistent pattern of behaviors and thoughts that extends to many aspects of a person's life.

Another myth is that people suffering from this disorder deliberately choose to avoid others because they don't like social interactions. In reality, many affected people have a deep desire to connect with others, but this desire is hampered by an intense fear of judgement and rejection. Their avoidance is not so much a choice as a defensive strategy against anticipated pain.

Some may also believe that this disorder is the result of a lack of willpower or strength of character. This idea is not only inaccurate but also harmful. It overlooks the fact that the disorder is rooted in complex biological, environmental and psychological factors. Reducing the condition to a lack of willpower prevents compassion and understanding.

There is also a misconception that avoidant personality disorder cannot be treated. Some believe that because it is a personality disorder, it is unchanging and ingrained in the very essence of the individual. However, research has shown that with proper intervention, symptoms can be alleviated and quality of life improved. The conviction that the disorder is unalterable can prevent affected individuals from seeking help or believing in their ability to change.

An additional myth is that all people with avoidant personality disorder are identical in their symptoms and behaviors. While some diagnostic criteria are required to make the diagnosis, the manifestation and intensity of symptoms can vary considerably from one person to another.

Additionally, it is unfortunately common to believe that people with this disorder are simply overprotective or constantly seeking others' approval. While reassurance-seeking can be a symptom, it is only one facet of a complex clinical picture.

Finally, some may think that avoidant personality disorder is caused by a single traumatic event. While traumatic events can play a role in the onset or exacerbation of symptoms, it would be simplistic to reduce the cause of the disorder to a single event. The reality is that the disorder is often the result of a combination of genetic, environmental and developmental factors.

Demystifying these misconceptions is essential. Myths and stereotypes, when unchecked, can perpetuate ignorance, reinforce stigma, and create barriers to understanding and treatment. By addressing these false ideas, we pave the way for better understanding, greater acceptance, and more effective interventions for those affected by avoidant personality disorder.

The Consequences of the Disorder on Daily Life

Despite its primarily psychological nature, avoidant personality disorder casts a long and persistent shadow over almost every aspect of the lives of those who suffer from it. Its influence is not limited to hesitancy in social interactions; it penetrates career, personal relationships, and, of course, mental health.

In everyday life, the omnipresence of interactions, responsibilities, and decisions can transform into a series of hurdles for someone with this disorder. What most consider routine tasks, such as going to a supermarket or answering a call, can be perceived as emotional trials. These situations, trivial for some, are mountains to climb for others.

The routine itself can be reshaped by the disorder. Choices are made to avoid certain situations, like using public transportation outside of peak hours or shopping at unusual times. These adjustments, which may seem insignificant at first glance, reflect the constant effort made by the person to adapt and navigate in a world that often seems hostile or, at least, threatening.

Professionally, avoidant personality disorder can be a significant hindrance. Interactions, whether with colleagues, superiors, or clients, are often inevitable. For someone suffering from this disorder, the prospect of these interactions can be a source of great anxiety. This fear of being judged or rejected can, as a result, affect active participation in meetings, defending ideas, or even seeking promotions or opportunities. Despite real skills and talents, an individual may feel held back in their professional progression by negative self-evaluation and self-imposed limitations.

Interpersonal relationships, whether in friendship or love, are also deeply affected. The fear of rejection can prevent the formation of new bonds or the strengthening of existing ones. Thus, the person may avoid engaging in new relationships or withdraw from a relationship at the slightest perceived tension. This defensive approach can make it difficult to establish deep and lasting relationships.

Mental health, of course, is directly influenced by this disorder. Constant avoidance, social withdrawal, and fear of judgment can generate or exacerbate other issues such as depression, anxiety, or even somatoform disorders. Psychological suffering is heightened by the feeling of isolation and the perception that the outside world is a threat. This constant state of alert can be exhausting and have repercussions on overall well-being.

In sum, avoidant personality disorder is not just a characteristic or personality trait. It is a complex condition that infiltrates almost every aspect of a person's life, altering their perception of the world and how they interact with it. To fully understand the impact of this disorder, it is essential to examine how it shapes the daily, professional, and relational reality of those who suffer from it.

Handbook of Applied Psychology

Accepting One's Diagnosis

Receiving a diagnosis of avoidant personality disorder can be disconcerting. The revelation that some of the fears, hesitations and avoidance behaviors are not simple personality traits, but rather manifestations of a recognized disorder, requires a period of adjustment. This adjustment is not a sign of weakness, but a natural process of awareness and acceptance.

A diagnosis, as intimidating as it may be, is above all a source of information. It provides a framework for understanding behaviors and feelings that previously may have seemed elusive or confusing. In the context of avoidant personality disorder, this means recognizing that the fear of rejection, sensitivity to criticism, or social withdrawal are not deliberate choices, but responses to internal and external stimuli.

The importance of accepting this diagnosis lies in its ability to open the door to appropriate interventions. Denying or minimizing the disorder can unnecessarily prolong distress and prevent the person from accessing resources or supports that could improve their quality of life. It is therefore less a resignation to a label than a recognition of the reality of one's condition.

It should be noted that acceptance does not mean passivity. On the contrary, it is the starting point for proactive action. By accepting their diagnosis, the individual gives themselves the possibility to learn more, to look for solutions, and to begin a process of adaptation. It also gives them the chance to define themselves not by the disorder, but by their ability to respond to it and manage its effects.

Acknowledging and accepting the diagnosis can also have a profound impact on self-esteem. Avoidant personality disorder, by its nature, can engender a negative self-image. Recognizing that these perceptions and behaviors are influenced by the disorder can provide some distance and a fresh perspective. This distance allows one to see that although the disorder is part of oneself, it does not define one's entire identity.

Additionally, accepting one's diagnosis can facilitate communication with others. By having a better understanding of what they are experiencing, individuals are better equipped to explain their feelings and behaviors to those around them, whether close ones, friends or professionals. This can help reduce misunderstandings and strengthen social ties, a crucial aspect for those who may feel isolated or misunderstood because of their disorder.

However, it is important to recognize that acceptance is a process, not a final state. There may be days of doubt, moments of resistance or periods of reflection. The important thing is to remember that every step towards acceptance, even if it seems small, is a step in the direction of understanding and well-being.

Ultimately, accepting a diagnosis of avoidant personality disorder is both a courageous and liberating act. It is acknowledging one's reality while opening up to the possibility of change and growth. It is an approach which, although complex, is essential to initiate the process of adaptation and healing.

Handbook of Applied Psychology

The First Step: Recognizing Your Fears

Recognizing your fears means confronting an integral part of your own being. For many suffering from avoidant personality disorder, life is a series of detours taken to avoid uncomfortable situations. But behind every detour often lies a fear or insecurity. By learning to identify them, we can start to shed the chains that hold us back.

Avoidant personality disorder is deeply rooted in fear. Fear of judgment, fear of rejection, fear of not measuring up. These fears may seem overwhelming, but their power largely lies in their ability to remain hidden, operating in the background. By bringing them to light, we can begin to strip them of this power.

Introspection is a powerful tool in this endeavor. Taking the time to sit in silence, breathe deeply, and delve into one's own thoughts can reveal surprising truths. It's not uncommon to discover, upon questioning why one hesitates to face a situation, a fear that had not been recognized as such until then.

Keeping a journal can also be helpful. By putting our thoughts and feelings into words, we give them form and structure, which can make fears more tangible and thus more manageable. Note the situations that provoke anxiety or fear and try to determine exactly what triggers these feelings.

Another way to identify your fears is to examine physical reactions. Fear is as much a physical phenomenon as an emotional one. A racing heart, excessive sweating, or a knotted stomach can all be indicators of an underlying fear. By paying attention to these signals, we can begin to understand what triggers them.

It's also helpful to consider worst-case scenarios. Asking oneself what could happen in the worst situation, and how one would react to it, can help put things into perspective. Often, by considering the worst, we realize that even that can be overcome.

Lastly, it's essential to remember that recognizing your fears is not a sign of weakness. On the contrary, it's an act of courage. It's far easier to continue avoiding them, taking detours, and never really facing what scares us. But by choosing to identify and understand these fears, we're making a bold decision in favor of our own growth and well-being.

It's only when we face our fears that we can begin to overcome them. And the first step in this process is to recognize them for what they are. Once that's done, the path to a more fulfilling life is opened.

Cultivating a Positive Self-Image

The image we have of ourselves is a fundamental element of our identity, influencing our interactions, our choices and the way we perceive the world around us. For those suffering from avoidant personality disorder, this image is often tainted with doubts and self-criticism that can undermine self-confidence and lead to avoidance behaviors. Cultivating a positive self-image is not just an act of affirmation, but a necessary step to overcome the limitations this disorder can impose.

The negative perception of self does not develop overnight. It is often the product of years of experiences, messages received from those around us, and the interpretations we make of the events in our lives. Reversing this perception therefore requires time, patience and a methodical approach.

One of the first steps towards a positive image is to identify and challenge negative beliefs about oneself. These are often generalizations based on isolated incidents, or criticisms that we have internalized. By taking the time to examine these beliefs, one can begin to see where they are inaccurate, and develop counterarguments to challenge them. For example, if one believes they are always awkward, they can remind themselves of the many times when they have acted competently and confidently.

Becoming aware of one's achievements is also fundamental. In the hustle and bustle of daily life, it's easy to forget everything one has accomplished. Taking the time to recognize and celebrate these achievements, whether big or small, can help reinforce self-esteem. This can range from completing a work project to small victories like talking to a stranger or voicing one's opinion.

Likewise, it is essential to learn to accept compliments. For those with low self-esteem, compliments can be difficult to accept, as they run counter to the negative image one has of oneself. However, learning to accept and integrate them can help reshape one's self-perception. Rather than minimizing or rejecting them, it is beneficial to welcome them and consider them as evidence contrary to what the inner critical voices might suggest.

Self-compassion is also a key element in boosting self-esteem. This means treating oneself with the same kindness, concern and understanding as one would treat a close friend. It is about recognizing that everyone makes mistakes, experiences failures, and goes through difficult times, without defining oneself by these experiences.

It is also advantageous to set and achieve realistic goals. This does not necessarily mean aiming low, but choosing goals that are both stimulating and achievable. Every goal achieved, even if modest, is further proof of one's abilities and reinforces self-confidence.

Finally, it is crucial to surround oneself with positive people who are supportive and affirming. The people we spend time with can have a significant impact on the image we have of ourselves. Distancing oneself from negative or critical people and seeking relationships that nourish and encourage can contribute to strengthening a positive self-image.

In short, cultivating a positive self-image is an ongoing process that requires both inner reflection and outward action. Every step taken towards this positive image not only reinforces self-esteem, but also opens the door to a more fulfilling and satisfying life.

Creating a Safe Environment

The perception of safety, both physical and emotional, is at the heart of our well-being. For those living with avoidant personality disorder, this sense of security can be fleeting or elusive due to the persistent fear of rejection, criticism, or judgment. Therefore, structuring one's environment to incorporate reassuring elements becomes crucial for managing and, eventually, overcoming the manifestations of this disorder.

The environment we're talking about encompasses everything: the physical space, the social circle, daily routines, and even the digital space. Each of these aspects plays a crucial role in the perception of safety and, consequently, in a person's ability to navigate the world despite their disorder.

Physical Space: Our living environment, whether it's our home, workplace, or other spaces we regularly frequent, greatly influences our state of mind. It's vital to arrange these spaces in a way that they are comfortable and reassuring. This might mean minimizing clutter, as a cluttered space can often be a source of stress. Personal items, soothing colors, soft lighting, plants, or natural elements can help create a serene atmosphere.

Social Circle: Social interactions are a double-edged sword for those with avoidant personality disorder. While a positive interaction can boost self-confidence, a negative experience can undermine it for an extended period. It's therefore essential to be selective about the people we allow into our lives. Surrounding oneself with kind, understanding, and positive people, and avoiding those who are critical, negative, or toxic is advisable. It can be beneficial to speak openly about one's disorder with close friends so they can offer tailored support.

Daily Routines: Routines provide structure and predictability, which can be reassuring. Simply knowing what to expect can often alleviate anxiety. Thus, establishing daily routines for meals, sleep, exercise, or hobbies is wise. These routines should not be rigid but rather serve as a general framework, offering some flexibility.

Digital Space: In our technological era, it's almost impossible to avoid the digital sphere. However, it can be a major source of anxiety, especially due to social media. Constant comparison, the potential for judgment or rejection, all this can exacerbate symptoms of avoidant personality disorder. It might be wise to limit time spent on these platforms, filter contacts, or even take digital breaks from time to time.

Another aspect to consider is setting boundaries. If certain environments or situations are particularly anxiety-inducing, it might be wise, where possible, to avoid them or find ways to make them less intimidating. For example, if large social gatherings are a source of anxiety, it might be better to favor smaller, more intimate meetings.

However, it's important to note that safety does not mean isolation. Cutting oneself off from the world is not the solution, as this would only reinforce fear and avoidance. The goal is to find a balance, where one feels safe without isolating from the enriching experiences and interactions life has to offer.

Creating a safe environment is an ongoing process, requiring adjustments based on needs and circumstances. Over time, a well-structured environment can become a solid foundation, allowing for the gradual challenging of fears and insecurities associated with avoidant personality disorder.

Learning Effective Communication

Communication is undoubtedly one of the most critical aspects of our daily interactions. It forms the basis of our relationships, whether personal, professional or social. For someone suffering from avoidant personality disorder, every conversation can feel like an obstacle course, dominated by the fear of judgment, rejection or criticism. It is in this context that developing communication skills becomes essential to break down those barriers and create authentic connections.

When it comes to communication, we often think of verbal expression. However, it is much more than that. It is an exchange, where listening plays an equally important role. Active listening, which involves being fully present and engaged in a conversation, allows not only to understand what the other person is saying, but also to grasp what they are feeling. In practice, this means maintaining eye contact, providing non-verbal cues such as nodding one's head, and asking questions to clarify or expand on a point.

On the other hand, expressing one's own feelings and needs is just as crucial. To do this, it is important to be clear and concise, use "I" statements rather than "you", and avoid placing blame. For example, instead of saying "You never listen to me", it would be more productive to say "I feel my concerns are not being heard when we talk". This nuance, although subtle, makes all the difference, because it expresses a personal feeling without accusing the other party.

Additionally, managing anxiety related to communication is another key element. Deep breathing, reminding oneself that every interaction is not an evaluation of one's self-worth, and practicing conversation in safer environments, such as with a close friend or therapist, can be beneficial steps.

That said, the reality is that communication does not always go smoothly. There will be misunderstandings, disagreements and uncomfortable moments. What matters is learning and growing from these experiences, apologizing when necessary, and constantly seeking to improve one's skills.

For people with avoidant personality disorder, the road to effective communication may seem long and winding. However, with practice, patience and a commitment to oneself, it is entirely possible to overcome these challenges and build enriching relationships. After all, communication is less a destination than an ongoing journey of learning and growth.

Handbook of Applied Psychology

Setting Achievable Goals

Living with avoidant personality disorder often means navigating a maze of emotions and insecurities, which can hinder personal fulfillment and the achievement of one's ambitions. However, these challenges don't have to define one's entire life. With a structured approach, it's possible to carve a path toward improvement. Setting achievable goals is a critical step in taking control of one's life and making progress.

Why is setting goals so crucial? Because they provide direction, meaning, and a framework for measuring progress. But it's not just about setting goals; it's about setting them smartly.

First, each goal should be specific. Saying "I want to be more social" is commendable, but it lacks clarity. In contrast, "I will start joining a discussion group or club once a month" offers a precise and measurable action.

Second, each goal should be measurable. This means you should be able to determine whether or not you've achieved this goal. In the example above, either you have joined a group or club, or you haven't. Measurement allows you to see where you stand and make necessary adjustments.

Third, the goal should be achievable. For someone who hasn't socialized for years due to their disorder, joining ten different groups might be overwhelming and even counterproductive. However, setting the goal to join just one group is not only achievable but also encouraging.

Fourth, the goal should be relevant. This means it should align with your current needs and desires. If you have no interest in joining a book club, for example, you're not obligated to do so. Your goals should resonate with what matters to you.

Lastly, each goal should be time-bound. This creates a sense of urgency and motivation. If you decide to join a group, set a deadline for doing so, such as "by the end of the month."

Once you've defined your goal using these criteria, it's vital to break it down into smaller, more manageable steps. These steps provide milestones, moments when you can celebrate your progress and adjust your approach if necessary. For instance, before joining a group, you might first research local groups that interest you, then make contact with one, then attend a first meeting. Each step taken brings you closer to your overall goal.

One of the major difficulties people with avoidant personality disorder face is the tendency to focus on their failures rather than their successes. This is where regularly tracking your goals comes into play. By noting your progress, even if minor, you can change this dynamic. You'll start to see that, despite the challenges, you are making headway.

Emotions, doubts, and fears will always be there. That's a reality of avoidant personality disorder. But with clearly defined goals and a structured approach to achieving them, these emotions can be managed. Ultimately, setting goals is not just about reaching external milestones but also about reclaiming one's life, learning to trust oneself, and moving forward at one's own pace.

It's a process, not a destination. Every small step, every goal achieved, builds self-confidence and provides tangible proof that change is possible. Setting achievable goals is an invitation to envision a future where avoidant personality disorder doesn't dictate every choice, but where you, with your aspirations and ambitions, are in control.

Asserting Oneself Confidently

Assertiveness is the ability to express oneself and defend one's rights without violating those of others. It is often contrasted with passivity or aggressiveness. For someone suffering from avoidant personality disorder, assertiveness can seem insurmountable. The fear of rejection, judgment or conflict can lead to a reluctance to speak up or set boundaries. However, it is possible to cultivate assertiveness by adopting suitable strategies and recognizing that this skill is essential for personal fulfillment and building healthy relationships.

One of the fundamental aspects of assertiveness is understanding one's own worth. Everyone has the right to speak up, have opinions and feelings, and set boundaries. This conviction is the foundation on which assertiveness is built. When we recognize our intrinsic value, it becomes easier to communicate our needs and desires to others.

It is also crucial to distinguish assertiveness from aggressiveness. Assertiveness is respectful of others and aims to establish open and honest communication. Aggressiveness, on the other hand, can hurt or dominate others. This distinction is essential to avoid slipping into behaviors that can alienate others or generate regret.

One of the first steps towards assertive communication is practicing active listening. This involves paying full attention to the other person, letting them know you understand what they are saying, and asking questions to clarify any points that seem unclear to you. Active listening demonstrates that you respect the other person and creates an environment conducive to open communication.

Expressing one's feelings and needs is also essential. Using "I" statements in communication is a simple yet effective technique. Instead of saying "You make me feel neglected", one could say "I feel neglected when we don't spend time together". This approach empowers the individual while avoiding blaming the other.

However, it is vital to remember that asserting oneself does not guarantee a positive outcome. Sometimes, despite all efforts to communicate clearly and respectfully, others may react defensively or negatively. In such situations, it is crucial to remember that you cannot control others' reactions, only how you choose to respond. It is perfectly acceptable to take a step back, breathe deeply, and opt to respond in a way that preserves your well-being.

Practice is the key to assertiveness. The more you train yourself to be assertive in different situations, the more natural it will become. This can start with simple actions like politely declining an invitation or voicing an opinion during a meeting. Over time, these actions will build your confidence and facilitate more complex interactions.

It is also beneficial to practice assertiveness in a safe environment. This could be with a therapist, coach or support group where you can simulate situations and receive constructive feedback. These scenarios will equip you with tools and strategies to handle real-life situations.

Additionally, visualization is a powerful technique for strengthening assertiveness. Picture yourself in a situation where you wish to be assertive. Visualize yourself speaking clearly, standing upright, maintaining eye contact, and voicing your needs. By regularly rehearsing this visualization, you will begin to internalize these behaviors and adopt them in reality.

Managing fear is also essential for developing assertiveness. Recognizing that fear is a normal emotion and should not dictate your behavior is a freeing realization. It is natural to feel anxiety at the idea of asserting oneself, especially if it has been a source of stress in the past. However, with practice and support, this fear can be alleviated.

Becoming assertive does not happen overnight. It is a process that requires commitment, practice and support. However, the benefits are well worth it. Assertiveness leads to healthier relationships, greater self-confidence, and better understanding of one's own needs and desires. It allows you to build a life where you can express yourself fully and authentically, without letting fear or doubt take over.

Handbook of Applied Psychology

Establishing Healthy Relationships

Interpersonal relationships play a central role in our daily lives, affecting our emotional, mental, and sometimes even physical well-being. For those living with avoidant personality disorder, relationships can be especially challenging. The fears of rejection, feelings of inferiority, or the belief of being inadequate can hinder the ability to establish and maintain healthy connections. Despite these challenges, it is entirely possible to create healthy and fulfilling relationships.

First, it's crucial to recognize the value of healthy relationships. Authentic and positive connections can provide emotional support, reduce feelings of isolation, and increase the sense of belonging and understanding. However, just like a garden requires regular attention to thrive, a healthy relationship needs care, patience, and effort to flourish.

Understanding what constitutes a healthy relationship is a good starting point. Healthy relationships are characterized by mutual respect, trust, honest communication, equality, and the ability to set boundaries. Both parties in a healthy relationship feel valued, heard, and supported.

Communication plays a pivotal role in any relationship. Having the ability to openly talk about one's feelings, concerns, and desires is crucial for establishing a trust-based relationship. This also includes the ability to actively listen to the other party, show empathy, and avoid judgmental or blaming behaviors. Regularly practicing assertiveness, as discussed in the previous chapter, can greatly improve communication.

Setting boundaries is also an essential component of healthy relationships. This means recognizing one's own needs and being able to communicate these needs to the other person. If you feel uncomfortable or overwhelmed by a situation, it's crucial to be able to express these feelings and set limits to protect your well-being.

It's also important to assess existing relationships. If a relationship consistently causes stress, pain, or anxiety, it may be time to reconsider that relationship. Sometimes, it may be necessary to end a toxic relationship or take a step back to protect oneself. It's crucial to surround oneself with people who support your growth and well-being.

However, establishing healthy relationships does not mean avoiding all conflict. Disagreements and misunderstandings are natural in any relationship. What's crucial is how these conflicts are managed. Approaching disagreements with an open attitude and willingness to understand the other's viewpoint can help resolve conflicts in a healthy and constructive manner.

Group activities or workshops can also offer opportunities to practice relational skills in a structured and supportive environment. These settings can help build confidence and provide constructive feedback on how to interact with others.

It's essential to recognize that every relationship is a journey, and there will be ups and downs. The key is to continue learning, growing, and adapting. Every interaction offers a chance to learn and improve. By focusing on personal growth, seeking support when necessary, and staying committed to the process, it's possible to develop and maintain healthy interpersonal relationships.

Over time and with practice, the ability to establish healthy relationships can greatly enhance one's quality of life. Despite the challenges posed by avoidant personality disorder, it is entirely possible to have enriching and rewarding relationships. The efforts invested in creating and maintaining these connections can have positive effects on overall well-being and offer a solid support network for overcoming future challenges.

The changing nature of relationships requires constant vigilance and a commitment to actively work on their improvement. But the rewards, in the form of deep connections, mutual support, and shared understanding, are invaluable. By placing relationships at the center of your priorities, being willing to invest time and energy, and approaching challenges with an open and positive attitude, you can overcome the obstacles posed by the disorder and establish healthy relationships that last.

Managing Rejection and Criticism

Navigating through today's social and professional world inevitably involves facing moments of rejection and criticism. While universal, these experiences can profoundly shake self-esteem, especially for those already struggling with emotional and psychological challenges. It is essential to recognize that although rejection and criticism may be painful, they do not define an individual's intrinsic worth. Additionally, they can provide opportunities for personal growth.

Rejection is often perceived as a negative judgment of our personality or abilities, but this interpretation is not always accurate. There are many reasons why rejection may occur, and many of them are out of our control. For example, an artist may have their work rejected by a gallery simply because it does not fit the theme of an exhibition, not because their work lacks value. Similarly, a job application may be turned down due to a multitude of factors, ranging from a company's specific needs to global economic dynamics.

Criticism, while it can be difficult to receive, functions differently. It often provides a window into how others perceive our work or actions. While some criticism may be spiteful or unconstructive, other feedback can provide valuable information to help refine a skill, adjust an approach, or see things from a different angle.

So how can we learn to navigate these often turbulent waters of rejection and criticism without disproportionately affecting our emotional well-being?

First, it can be helpful to separate our sense of identity from the specific experience of rejection or criticism. Rather than identifying with the experience, view it as an isolated event which, while painful, does not encapsulate all of who you are or what you're worth.

Next, try to take a step back and objectively evaluate the situation. Ask yourself contextual questions. Is this rejection truly a measure of your worth or is it the result of external factors over which you have little or no control? Is the criticism you received based on factual observations, or is it the expression of a personal opinion?

Learning not to take things personally is a skill that takes time and practice, but it's essential for navigating a world where rejection and criticism are commonplace. It can also be helpful to surround yourself with trusted people who can offer outside perspectives, help contextualize rejection or criticism, and provide emotional support.

It's also crucial to remember that every experience, whether positive or negative, provides an opportunity for learning. Perhaps a rejection may lead you to reconsider an approach, rethink an idea, or redirect yourself towards a path more aligned with your goals and aspirations. Criticism, when handled constructively, can be the springboard towards self-improvement and growth.

Finally, remember that emotional well-being is a journey, and like any other journey, there will be highs and lows. What matters most is not the experience itself, but how we choose to respond to it. By learning to approach rejection and criticism with an open, thoughtful and constructive mindset, we can not only strengthen our resilience, but also evolve and grow as individuals.

Roles and Boundaries

Living in a complex society often involves juggling multiple roles at once. Whether it's our role within the family, at work, in the community or in friendships, each of these roles has its own expectations, responsibilities and demands. Likewise, as we go through different life stages, we find ourselves facing changing challenges, evolving expectations and growing or shifting responsibilities. To stay grounded, balanced, and not feel overwhelmed, it is essential to clearly define our roles and boundaries.

Defining one's roles means understanding what is expected of us in a given context. This can include explicit responsibilities like caring for children or managing a work project, but also implicit expectations like being there to listen to a friend or actively participating in community life. By clearly understanding what each of these roles requires, we are better equipped to prepare for them, manage our time and resources, and deal with any challenges that arise.

However, defining roles is not enough. It is just as crucial to set boundaries. Boundaries are the invisible but vital barriers we establish to safeguard our mental, emotional and physical well-being. They help us determine what we are willing to accept or refuse, what we are willing to do or not do, and how we want others to treat us.

Without clearly established boundaries, we risk overextending ourselves, feeling frustrated, exhausted or resentful, and compromising our wellness. For instance, if we don't set boundaries in our parenting role, we could end up constantly sacrificing our own needs for those of our kids, which over time could lead to burnout. Or without clear boundaries in a friendship or romantic relationship, we might feel trapped in an imbalanced pattern of give and take, where we constantly give without receiving anything back.

The importance of setting boundaries also manifests itself in the professional sphere. By establishing boundaries around work hours, responsibilities and expectations, we can maintain work-life balance, avoid professional burnout and safeguard our mental health.

So how can we effectively define our roles and boundaries so as not to feel overwhelmed?

It's useful to start with self-assessment. Ask yourself questions about what you expect from yourself in each role, what is expected of you, and what you are realistically capable of giving. It's important to remember we are human beings with limited capabilities, and acknowledging those limitations is not a sign of weakness but of wisdom.

Once we have a better grasp of our roles, it's time to define our boundaries. This can be as simple as saying «no» when asked to take on an additional task at work, or as complex as redefining expectations in a long-term relationship. Setting boundaries is an ongoing process that requires open, honest communication and, above all, self-respect.

Defining one's roles and limits is also an exercise in autonomy. It's recognizing that while we may want to meet every expectation and shoulder every responsibility, we also have the right and responsibility to safeguard our wellness. By deliberately choosing where and how we devote our time and energy, we regain control over our lives.

Ultimately, defining our roles and boundaries is an act of self-care. It is acknowledging our worth, our needs and our capabilities, and making the necessary choices to live a balanced, fulfilling, authentic life. In doing so, we not only protect ourselves but also set an example for those around us, encouraging them to do the same for their own well-being.

Surrounding Yourself with Support

In the context of modern life, it's crucial to understand that no one is an island. The challenges life presents can sometimes seem overwhelming, but they become more manageable with a reliable support network. This network can be a mix of friends, family, colleagues, and professionals who offer comfort, advice, and, in some cases, tangible resources.

Support comes in many forms, ranging from empathetic listening to sharing resources and expertise. Sometimes, just knowing someone is there for you, that you are not alone in your situation, can make all the difference. Yet, building such a network takes time, effort, and sincere communication.

It often starts with family and friends, the pillars of any personal support network. This can include parents, siblings, partners, or long-standing friends. They are often the first to witness our struggles and can offer both an external perspective and the comfort of familiarity. Talking to these individuals, sharing your feelings and concerns, can often lead to unexpected solutions or, at the very least, a sense of relief.

Beyond this inner circle, colleagues and peers can also be an important source of support, especially for challenges related to career or education. In many professions, there are support groups or associations that offer a platform for sharing experiences, asking questions, and getting advice.

There are also times when professional support is necessary. Therapists, counselors, and other mental health professionals can offer valuable expertise to help navigate complex situations. Their specialized training allows them to provide specific strategies and tools to cope with a variety of challenges.

But how does one cultivate a support network? First, it's essential to recognize the value of support and be open to receiving it. This sometimes requires overcoming pride or reluctance to share personal problems. This step is crucial because support can only be effective if one is receptive to it.

Next, investing time and effort in your relationships is important. This means nurturing relationships, checking in on how others are doing regularly, and being there for them in turn. Support is reciprocal: the more you give, the more you receive.

Furthermore, it's also crucial to expand your network. Participating in social groups, clubs, professional associations, or workshops can be an excellent way to meet new people and add extra layers to your support network.

Finally, communication is key. Being clear about what you need, actively listening, and giving feedback are all essential to effective communication. The clearer you can express your needs and feelings, the more likely you are to receive the kind of support you're looking for.

In conclusion, a solid support network is essential for navigating the complexities of modern life. Whether you're going through a difficult period or simply looking to enhance your overall well-being, surrounding yourself with supportive people can make all the difference.

Handbook of Applied Psychology

Managing Crisis Moments

Life, with all its nuances and complexities, inevitably confronts us with difficult times, crises that can shake our foundations. Whether it's a sudden loss, trauma, major confrontation or any other distressing event, it is crucial to have tools to navigate through these storms. Although each crisis has its particularities, there are general strategies that can help cope and regain a sense of stability.

First, it is paramount to acknowledge the impact of a crisis. Moments of great distress can have repercussions on mental, emotional and even physical health. There may be a temptation to minimize or ignore the gravity of a situation, especially for those used to being perceived as «strong» or «unshakeable.» Yet recognition is the first step towards taking constructive action.

Acknowledging a crisis does not mean dwelling on it or drowning in it. It simply means understanding that an event or series of events has disrupted your usual equilibrium. With this recognition, you can begin assessing what you need to get back on your feet.

One of the first steps in coping with a crisis is to seek out a safe space. If the crisis stems from a dangerous situation, it is imperative to remove yourself from that situation or find shelter. This could mean physically withdrawing or, in the case of emotional or mental crises, finding a place where you can be sheltered from outside stimuli in order to take a moment to pull yourself together.

Once in a safe place, breathe. This may seem simple, even simplistic, but conscious, deep breathing has the power to anchor the body and mind. It brings oxygen to the brain, allowing for clearer thinking and decreasing the immediate "fight or flight" response that can accompany a crisis.

Speaking to someone you trust is another critical step. Sharing what you're feeling and experiencing can lighten the burden of the situation. It's not necessarily about finding immediate solutions, but simply verbalizing your feelings and experiences. This can provide valuable clarity and, often, simply being heard can be incredibly therapeutic.

When facing a crisis, it can be tempting to seek quick fixes or escapes. While some of these solutions may offer temporary relief, they usually don't address the deeper root cause of the crisis. It is therefore essential to resist the urge to rely on unhealthy coping mechanisms. These can include, but aren't limited to, excessive alcohol or drug use, complete avoidance or denial.

Instead, try surrounding yourself with positive reminders and affirmations. Recalling past successes or personal strengths can provide a foundation to lean on during moments of self-doubt or vulnerability. While this may seem insufficient in the face of a crisis' gravity, these reminders can serve as lifelines, helping recall that we've made it through difficult times before.

Another aspect to consider is perspective. Although extremely difficult during a crisis moment, trying to view the situation within a broader context can help reduce the immediate intensity of pain or distress. This doesn't mean minimizing the situation but rather contextualizing it.

Let's not forget the importance of self-care during these times. This includes healthy eating, periods of rest and, if possible, physical activity. These elements may seem disconnected from the crisis itself but they play a crucial role in mood stabilization and providing the necessary resources to cope.

Finally, don't hesitate to seek professional support if needed. Sometimes a crisis' severity exceeds what we're able to handle on our own or with our personal support system. Therapists, counselors and other mental health professionals are trained to help individuals navigate through these tumultuous times, offering strategies and tools to overcome and eventually find meaning or growth from the experience.

In short, coping with crisis is an arduous ordeal but with the right strategies and support, it is possible to navigate through it. Every crisis presents an opportunity, however hard to see in the moment. With time, support and proper care, these difficult moments can ultimately lead to greater resilience and deeper self-understanding.

The Importance of Routine

In a world where everything seems to be in constant motion and the unexpected can arise at any moment, finding some semblance of order can be not only comforting but essential for mental well-being. A daily routine, no matter how simple, can become a solid anchor in the turbulent waters of life, especially for those living with a disorder. By delving into the intricacies of routine and its importance, we discover how it can serve as a valuable tool for overcoming challenges and restoring internal balance.

What is a routine, and why is it so powerful? A routine is essentially a set of actions or activities performed repeatedly, usually at specific times of the day. It can be as basic as brushing your teeth every morning or as complex as following a precise schedule of exercise, meditation, work, and leisure. The power of routine lies in its ability to instill a sense of predictability in an otherwise unpredictable life.

When dealing with disorders, whether emotional, mental, or physical, a common experience is a loss of control. This may be due to unpredictable symptoms, unexpected emotional reactions, or just a general sense of being unmoored. In this context, routine can act as a shield against unpredictability. By establishing familiar activities that occur at set times, we create anchor points throughout the day.

These anchor points, or moments of routine, can help divide the day into manageable segments. Instead of viewing the day as a vast ocean of uncertainty, it becomes a series of smaller streams, each with its own beginning, middle, and end. This segmentation can help reduce anxiety and provide a sense of achievement as each segment is navigated.

Routine is also crucial for establishing healthy habits. For instance, someone suffering from insomnia might benefit from a bedtime routine. By establishing a series of actions to perform before going to sleep, such as reading a book or having a cup of herbal tea, the brain begins to associate these actions with sleep, thus easing the transition to restful slumber.

Moreover, for those who might feel overwhelmed by negative or intrusive thoughts, routine offers constructive distraction. Instead of being swept away by mental spirals, focusing on the task at hand helps to recenter the mind. It's a way of training the brain to concentrate on the present rather than getting lost in worries or regrets.

Consider another example: someone struggling with depression might find it hard to muster the motivation to start their day. Here, a minimal morning routine can help overcome that initial inertia. Getting up, stretching, opening the curtains to let in light—these are small steps that can help set a more positive dynamic in motion for the rest of the day.

It's also important to note that the benefit of routine lies not only in the actions it entails but also in the sense of mastery it provides. Completing a task, any task, often brings a sense of accomplishment. For someone grappling with a disorder, this feeling of self-efficacy can be powerfully restorative.

However, while acknowledging the benefits of routine, it's also crucial to incorporate some flexibility. There may be days when following the routine to the letter is impossible or undesirable. In such moments, it's essential not to blame oneself or feel that all is lost. The beauty of routine also lies in its ability to be picked up where it was left off.

Ultimately, routine is less about a rigid set of actions and more about a canvas of stability to rely upon. By deliberately integrating moments of routine into the day, we offer a counterpoint to uncertainty, a way to assert some control, and a means to nurture habits that support well-being. In the battle against disorders, it's a silent but powerful ally, bringing order and stability to an often chaotic world.

Handbook of Applied Psychology

The Benefits of Movement

The human body is a wonder of nature, a well-oiled machine that, when in motion, can accomplish incredible things. Movement, or physical activity, is intrinsic to our nature. Since the earliest days of humankind, we have run, jumped, danced, and done whatever was necessary to survive. But today, as many people face various disorders, the importance of movement in managing and overcoming these conditions is more relevant than ever.

When we talk about physical activity, it's crucial to clarify that this does not necessarily mean lifting heavy weights or running marathons. The simple act of getting up and walking, or stretching in the morning, is already a form of physical activity. It's this variety of options that makes movement so accessible to everyone, regardless of their current fitness level.

One of the most obvious benefits of movement is its direct impact on physical health. Regular movement strengthens the cardiovascular system, improves lung capacity, promotes bone density, and builds muscle. These physical enhancements, while essential in themselves, also have beneficial effects on disorder management.

A robust cardiovascular system, for example, ensures blood is being pumped efficiently throughout the body, delivering essential oxygen and nutrients to cells. This can improve cognitive function and maintain a healthy brain, which is critical for those who may be facing mental or emotional disorders. The brain, after all, is an organ, and like any other organ, it benefits from a healthy supply of oxygen and nutrients.

Additionally, physical activity stimulates the release of various hormones and neurotransmitters. One of the most notable is dopamine, often dubbed the "happiness hormone." Dopamine plays a key role in feelings of pleasure and reward. For those living with depression or anxiety, for instance, this boost of dopamine can provide temporary relief from symptoms and mood enhancement.

On top of dopamine, movement also induces the release of endorphins, peptides that act as natural painkillers. Endorphins can help alleviate physical pain but they also have an effect on mood, provoking a feeling of euphoria that is often described as a "runner's high." This state can be incredibly beneficial for those who often feel overwhelmed by their disorders.

Movement, especially when performed outdoors, also provides the chance to reconnect with the world around us. Walking through a park, biking along a trail or simply practicing deep breathing exercises in the sunshine can help establish a sense of connection with nature. This connection is often cited as having therapeutic effects, allowing the individual to feel grounded and in tune with the world around them.

In addition to biological advantages, physical activity can also provide a sense of accomplishment. Reaching a goal, however small, can give self-esteem a significant boost. For someone struggling with a disorder, this feeling of achievement can be a precious reminder of their own strength and ability to overcome challenges. Every step taken, every movement made, is a victory in itself, bolstering self-confidence and self-determination.

It's also important to mention the social aspect of movement. Joining a walking club, taking dance classes or simply going on strolls with a friend are all opportunities to interact with others. These social interactions can be beneficial to break the isolation some people dealing with a disorder may feel. Feeling supported and understood by a community can be an essential factor to make it through difficult periods.

However, it's crucial to note that while physical activity offers many benefits, it is not a panacea. It should be considered as part of a holistic approach to manage and overcome the disorder. Each individual must find the type and level of activity that suits them best. It's always advisable to consult a healthcare professional or therapist before embarking on a new physical activity regime, especially if the individual has particular concerns or preexisting conditions.

Ultimately, movement is a powerful tool in the toolkit of anyone seeking to manage a disorder. It offers both physical and mental benefits and while it may not be the solution to every problem, it can play a crucial role in helping individuals feel better, both in their bodies and in their minds. Embracing movement means embracing life itself.

Adapting Your Lifestyle

When it comes to well-being and mental health, lifestyle plays a pivotal role. It's not just about what we do, but also how, when, and why we do it. Our lifestyle is the sum of the choices we make each day, and together, these choices determine the quality of our existence.

The environment we operate in, our routines, our diet, our level of physical activity, the people we choose to spend time with—all shape our daily experience. Therefore, adapting our lifestyle to promote well-being requires attention to these various elements.

Starting by asking ourselves what truly matters is essential. What brings us joy, satisfaction, and a sense of achievement? The answers will provide a roadmap for directing necessary changes.

The organization of our day is central. When we wake up, how we start our day, the activities we choose to undertake first, all this can influence our mood for the hours to come. Simple moments, like taking the time to enjoy a good breakfast, or allowing ourselves a few minutes of silent contemplation, can have a profound impact on our mindset.

The environment in which we spend most of our time, usually our home, also plays a significant role. A bright, airy, and organized space can enhance our mental well-being. This doesn't necessarily mean making big changes, but sometimes simple adjustments, like rearranging furniture or adding decorative elements that please us, can make all the difference.

Technology has become an omnipresent part of our lives. While it offers numerous benefits, it can also be a source of stress and distraction. Allocating moments when we disconnect from our devices can be beneficial. It's not about avoiding technology but using it in a conscious and intentional way.

Diet is another central pillar of our lifestyle. The foods we consume affect not only our physical health but also our mood and energy. Educating oneself, experimenting, and finding a diet that suits one's individual needs can be a journey in itself, but the benefits are well worth it.

Finally, relationships play a huge role in our well-being. The people with whom we choose to share our time can either lift us up or pull us down. Cultivating healthy, nourishing, and mutually beneficial relationships is crucial.

In summary, adapting your lifestyle is a dynamic process. It's not about reaching a final destination but rather engaging in a journey of continuous learning and growth. Every small choice, every conscious decision, brings us closer to the desired well-being. And even though this path requires effort, the rewards—in the form of health, happiness, and fulfillment—are well worth it.

Recognizing Signs of Relapse

Relapse, or the return of a disorder after a period of improved well-being or remission, is a reality that many people have to face in their healing journey. However, it does not mean failure or the end of the road. Recognizing early warning signs of relapse can allow for quick action, prevent further deterioration, and regain the path to recovery.

It's essential to keep in mind that relapse symptoms can vary among individuals and disorder types. However, some key indicators can be monitored.

Change in sleep habits is one of the most common signs of mental or emotional imbalance. A person may either have trouble falling or staying asleep, or sleep excessively. Sleep is crucial for mental health, and prolonged disruptions can signal an issue.

Appetite is another indicator. Eating too much or too little, or noticing drastic changes in food cravings, may denote trouble. Eating and mental health are closely linked, and any disturbance in this area warrants attention.

Social withdrawal is also a red flag. If a previously sociable person starts avoiding interactions, frequently canceling appointments, or generally seems less interested in relationships, it may be an indication of relapse.

Neglecting personal care, like disregarding personal hygiene, not caring for appearance, or abandoning usual routines can also be a tell-tale. These changes can reflect lowering self-esteem or depressive moods.

Lack of motivation or loss of interest in previously enjoyed activities can also raise concern. Whether it's a hobby, work, or simply taking pleasure in daily life, a sudden decrease in engagement could mean something is not right.

A change in energy level should also be monitored. This may manifest as constant fatigue, lack of energy, or on the contrary, hyperactivity or restlessness.

The tendency to avoidance is another sign. Avoiding situations, places or people associated with unpleasant or traumatic memories could denote returning symptoms.

Negative thinking or repetitive thought patterns can also act as warning lights. An increase in negative thinking, rumination or excessive worrying may indicate mental imbalance.

Additionally, heightened emotional sensitivity or reactivity whether to anger, sadness or anxiety can flag relapse. Strong, uncontrolled emotions may signal a need for intervention.

It's also crucial to take any self-harming speech or behavior seriously. Even if they seem mild or sporadic, they can be indicators of deep distress.

Of course, not all these signs necessarily mean imminent relapse. However, vigilance in recognizing them is important. Identifying potential relapse as early as possible allows for quick intervention. This may involve treatment adjustment, consulting a healthcare professional, or simply taking time for oneself. In any case, recognizing the signs is the first step to ensure continued wellness and progress on the healing path.

Handbook of Applied Psychology

Continuing to Challenge Yourself

Evolution is a continuous process. Just as a tree keeps growing as it stretches its branches and deepens its roots, personal growth is fueled by the constant effort to go beyond what is known and comfortable. Challenge, exploration, and expanding personal boundaries are essential for moving beyond stagnation and finding renewal in life, regardless of the personal challenges or disorders one faces.

Humans are, by nature, adaptable beings. This adaptability has allowed us to overcome countless challenges throughout history, be they environmental, social, or personal. However, this adaptability is a double-edged sword. On one hand, it allows us to adjust and find balance in new situations; on the other, it can also lead to stagnation if we get too comfortable in our comfort zone.

Finding oneself in a comfort zone is often comforting. After all, it's a space where everything is familiar, predictable, and relatively free of threats. Yet, if we linger too long in this familiarity, we risk becoming resistant to change, losing our natural curiosity, and closing ourselves off to new experiences. This is where the danger lies: in stagnation and complacency.

So, why is it so important to continue challenging oneself? The answer lies in how the brain and body react to new situations. When faced with a new situation or challenge, the brain is stimulated to find solutions, thus creating new neural connections. These connections strengthen brain plasticity, helping the brain stay sharp and agile. Moreover, overcoming new challenges boosts self-confidence and resilience, qualities essential for dealing with life's ups and downs.

It's also worth noting that challenging oneself doesn't necessarily mean taking reckless risks or putting oneself in danger. It can be as simple as learning a new skill, diving into a new book, exploring a new culture, or opening oneself up to different perspectives. It's about embracing change and novelty, keeping an open mind, and continuing to learn.

Regularly challenging oneself also keeps us connected to ourselves and the world around us. In a constantly changing world, it's easy to feel overwhelmed or disconnected if one doesn't adapt or evolve along with it. By making it a habit to challenge oneself, we develop an adaptability that allows us to remain relevant and engaged in the world around us.

Overcoming personal challenges, whether it's managing a health condition, facing trauma, or overcoming addiction, also requires a constant commitment to challenge oneself. Even after achieving a certain level of stability or well-being, the journey doesn't stop there. To ensure lasting healing and well-being, it's crucial to continue looking for ways to grow, flourish, and strengthen oneself.

In the end, continuing to challenge oneself is a celebration of life itself. Each new challenge, each new experience, is an opportunity to grow, learn, and further flourish. And even if every challenge doesn't immediately bring success or satisfaction, each effort brings us closer to our highest potential. By recognizing this truth, embracing challenge, and constantly striving to go beyond what is known and comfortable, we honor not only our own journey but also the very fabric of life and evolution.

Conclusion

Living with a disorder, whether psychological, emotional or physical, is never easy. Dark days can seem endless, challenges insurmountable. But at the heart of this battle, there is a spark, an inner strength that allows you to keep moving forward, even when everything seems to be against you. This spark is fueled by acknowledging progress made and celebrating victories, however small they may be.

Every day lived is proof of resilience. Every moment of happiness, however fleeting, is a victory over the disorder. It is essential to recognize these moments and celebrate them. For it is by celebrating the small wins that one finds the strength to continue the battle, to keep moving forward, despite the obstacles and challenges.

One of the keys to living fully, even in the presence of a disorder, is to cultivate an attitude of gratitude. Being thankful for the little things, the moments of joy, the laughter shared, the accomplishments, even if they seem trivial. This gratitude is like a balm for the soul, it soothes the pain and brightens the dark moments.

Additionally, it is essential to surround oneself with people who understand, support and encourage. Friends, family, therapists or support groups can be an invaluable source of comfort and motivation. They can help put things in perspective, remind you of progress made, and celebrate victories. Their presence, listening and backing can make all the difference during difficult times.

It is also important to remember the path to healing and wellness is not linear. There will be ups and downs, breakthroughs and setbacks. And that is normal. What matters is not the destination but the journey. And every step forward, even when followed by two steps back, is proof of strength, courage and determination.

Remembering too that the disorder does not define who you are is crucial. It is part of your story, your journey, but not your identity. You are so much more than your disorder. You are a unique individual, with dreams, passions, talents and qualities. You have the ability to love, laugh, create, dream and make those dreams a reality. Never let the disorder make you forget that.

Every day is a new opportunity. An opportunity to get up, face your fears, overcome obstacles, and live fully. This does not mean ignoring the reality of the disorder but rather choosing not to be defined by it. Choosing to see beyond the limitations imposed by the disorder and recognize the infinite possibilities open to you.

And lastly, don't forget to take care of yourself. This can mean different things for different people. It could be taking time to rest, meditate, engage in an activity you love, or simply take a moment for yourself. What matters is recognizing your needs and taking the necessary steps to meet them. Because it is by taking care of yourself that you will find the strength to keep moving forward, despite the challenges.

In summary, living fully despite a disorder is an act of courage, resilience and determination. It means choosing to see beyond limitations, celebrate victories, acknowledge progress made, and surround oneself with support. It is, ultimately, choosing life with everything it entails of joys, challenges, tears and laughter. And it is this choice, this courage to live fully, that makes every day a victory in itself.